When the Impossible Becomes Reality

A Journal for Parents to Feel Confident When Communicating with Schools

When the Impossible Becomes Reality

Scan the QR code to connect with Andrena.

Dedication

I dedicate this book to Christ who strengthens me daily. To my son who was given to me by God as a gift to use as a measure for the encouragement to give back to society and my community.

To my daughter who is my minnie me (the trooper), my husband who gave me the support during my dark days when I thought things were impossible, my mother who gave birth to me and provided me with an opportunity that I am so grateful for, and to my dad, the person who instill values, and all the ethics that I continuously display daily.

A special thank you to one of my teachers Ms. Dorothy Hill. She gave me the encouragement when I needed it most because I thought math (Arithmetic) was impossible for me to do; you helped me to get through those difficult times for me to get my "Aha" moments.

"It always seems impossible until it's done"
– Nelson Mandela

TABLE OF CONTENTS

This journal will empower parents that want to advocate for their child at school. Please use the information, activity sheets and journal pages to become more actively involved.

Introduction

I created this book and journal to encourage teachers and parents to let them know that nothing is impossible when you put all that you can into it. The feeling of accomplishment is one of the greatest you can ever have when you can look back at the fruits of your labor.

We are ALL faced with obstacles and challenges, but it is the endurance and the mindset to make the change. BE WILLING TO MAKE THAT CHANGE!!!!!!

Aha Moments "When They Get It"

a. Fluency
b. Comprehension
c. Building confidence in the classroom

"I can't is a sluggard who is too lazy to try". These are the words that my teacher, Ms. Hill, would say daily. When I face obstacles, these words play over and over in my head.

Aha Moments "When They Get It"

According to the Merriam-Webster.com, Aha moment-"a moment of sudden realization, inspiration, insight, recognition, or comprehension. The aha moment you experience when you've been trying to remember the name of a song and three hours later it hits you". This is the moment when your students suddenly get it. The "it" is what you have been teaching for the past couple of days or weeks and it seems as if they cannot fathom what you are talking about.

Aha Moments "When They Get It"

Every day is a new day, and it is a new start; but at the end you must reflect and ask yourself "What am I doing wrong that my students cannot get it?" YES, it again.

You have tried everything that you have in you and then one day you tell a story about an event or a scenario and then they get the "IT". This is when you ask yourself if there are things that I must do for the students so that they won't have moments of frustration when they cannot seem to understand what you are trying to impart to them daily, but rather find things they can connect to, whether an event or a story.

Aha Moments "When They Get It"

As teachers, we must find inventive ways to reach the students daily. Fluency is defined as the ability to read with speed, accuracy, and proper expression. When reading aloud, fluent readers read in phrases and add intonation (reading with emphasis and expression) appropriately. Their reading is smooth and has an expression~ Reading Rocket. There are other parts of reading before fluency such as phonemic awareness, letter knowledge, and concepts of print. Once the main components are mastered, then comprehension can be successful.

Aha Moments "When They Get It"

Comprehension is the understanding and interpretation of what is read. To be able to accurately understand written material, children need to be able to:

(1) decode what they read

(2) make connections between what they read and what they already know

(3) think deeply about what they have read.

Aha Moments "When They Get It"

It is important to know there are 9 components of reading. These are listed below: we will focus on the first five, which are the most impactful for new readers, in my professional opinion.

- Phonetic awareness/ letter knowledge and concepts of print
- Alphabetic code (phonics and decoding)
- Automatic reading of text
- Vocabulary
- Text comprehension
- Reading expression
- Writing... spelling, handwriting, speed...
- Screening and continuous assessment
- Motivate and literacy horizons

Aha Moments "When They Get It"

We must build confidence in the students by encouraging them daily even when you as the teacher know there are obstacles. With daily encouragement, they will try their hardest. Do not be quick to tell them that they are wrong after answering a question; instead, try asking probing questions that will eventually lead them to the answer. So, if you must ask again and again, then it's best. Some children shut down when they are told that they are wrong as it may hurt their self-esteem because that is all they have been hearing all their lives. Be the one to make a change in their lives. If you only reach one per year, then that is fine.

Aha Moments "When They Get It"

School may be the only place they are encouraged or feel some sense of love and care. I can remember what one of my teachers (Ms. Hill) did for me. Math was my greatest challenge because I told myself that it was hard. She took me under her wings and worked with me day in and day out until I was able to understand it. Math was my greatest fear; I just had a mental block for math because it seemed very difficult. As an adult, I can now look back and determine that I could not remember the formula and the rules for working out the problems. She just ensured that I followed the formulas. Now, math is my strongest subject.-"Someone cared".

Aha Moments "When They Get It"

Use the venn diagram below to compare your parents' relationship with your teachers vs yours with your child's teacher.

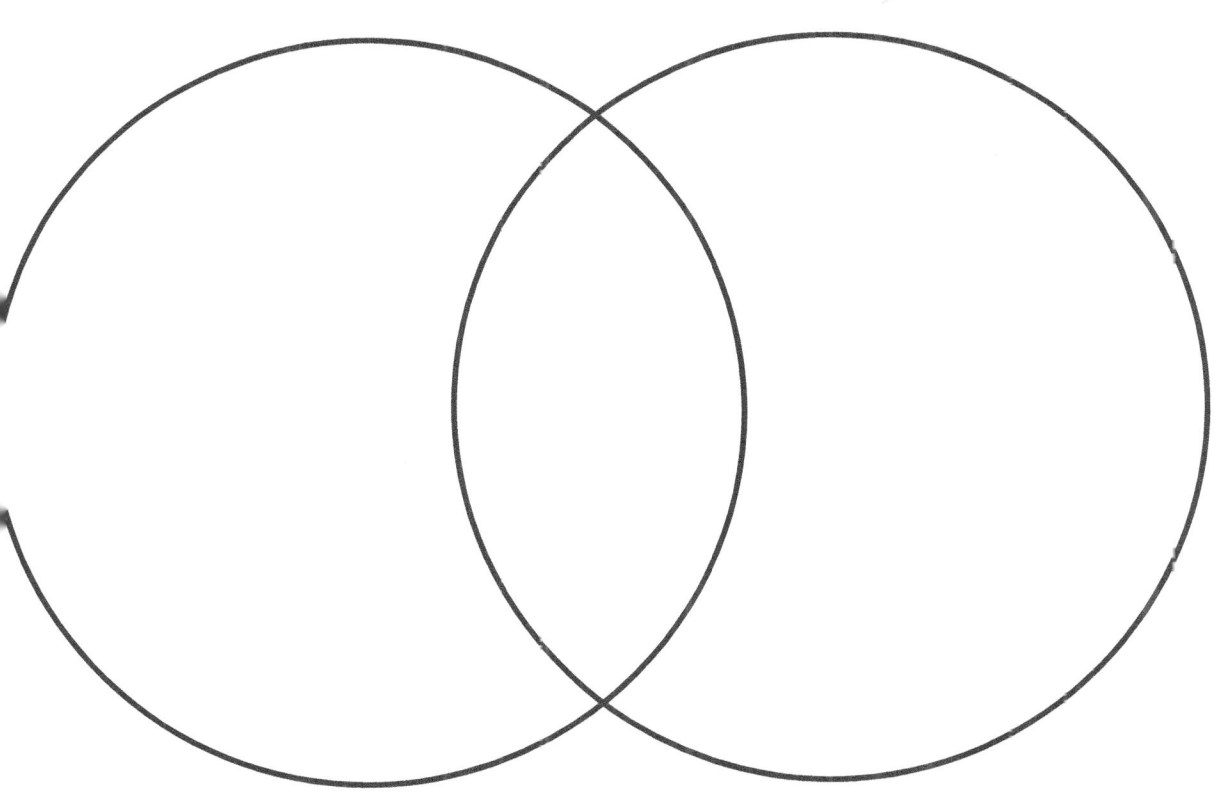

Aha Moments "When They Get It"

You can't go back and change the beginning, start where you are, and change the ending- C. S. Lewis.

Sense of Accomplishment

- Teaching philosophy
- Ways to give back to the community
- What not to do... learning from frustration with mistakes from the school system

Please share this section "Sense of Accomplishment" with your child's teacher. This is a great way to foster a positive relationship.

Sense of Accomplishment

How good does it feel when you accomplish something? My teaching philosophy "All children can learn and will learn". It does not matter if they have special needs or not- they can learn. We must find out how they learn. Using the Multiple Intelligence Theory by Howard Gardner certainly will help to know and understand the various types of learner you have in your class and help use them to find areas for success. When your student can complete a task, "Do you ever wonder that they have a feeling of accomplishment?" It is such an awesome feeling to be successful!

Sense of Accomplishment

Give them the credit when they do; celebrate individual accomplishment, it might inspire others to work a little harder and put out more effort. That is another "AHA" moment.

You can give back to the community by teaching in the neighborhood schools or tutoring a child. Remember when teachers did that and everyone knew them? We must go back to the basics, it worked, and teachers were well respected and held to a high standard. "Where did it go"? Let us get back to the good old-fashioned ways of teaching, it is the profession you have chosen. Think about why you chose it and put your all in it. Let's encourage each other to take back control of the classroom.

Sense of Accomplishment

What should you do if YOU believe the school system has failed you and your child-stop pointing the finger or playing the blame game. Instead, find other interventions. Do your research and look for and find programs to help the child; first, look to see if it's already in the school system and talk to someone to see if your child is qualified for these programs. At times, there are already up and running programs your child can benefit from; try to find how they can get in. RESEARCH, RESEARCH, RESEARCH !!!

Progress Towards Literacy

- Smart Goal Planning
- Focus on the past successes, do not live in the moment of frustration.
- Partnering with the schools

Progress Towards Literacy

Set goals for the students-they must be realistic and attainable. You can make long-term goals but set smaller goals or steps to get to the long-term goals. What can they accomplish by the end of the school year? It works!!!!! Think about a child reaching his or her growth milestones. Always plan, you must know where your students are at the beginning of the school year and what their strengths and weaknesses are. Analyze the data!!!

Progress Towards Literacy

Reach them where they are and build for later transfer. At the time, it may seem very difficult. This is when you ask yourself, "How am I going to do this?" Start somewhere, ideas will come eventually. Collaborate with your peers, at times you cannot do it ALL by yourself. Get help when needed. According to Steven Covey, *start with the end in mind.*

Progress Towards Literacy

Think about all the success you've had in life. You work very hard to get there. The success-is the accomplishment of an aim or purpose.

Do not forget that there is a thin line between success and failure. Keep your eyes on the prize. "Remember that there are many pitfalls on your way to success and this is where the frustration comes in" C.S. Lewis. Push forward as hard as you can and overlook the distractions, it will be okay. "Remember that hard work is not the road to success, you need the right planning" C.S. Lewis.

Progress Towards Literacy

Plan effectively and execute the plan with fidelity. Nothing is impossible if you only believe! Be prepared to change your mindset if you want to succeed. "*You should never view your challenges as a disadvantage. Instead, you need to understand that your experience facing and overcoming adversity is one of your biggest advantages*" First Lady Michelle Obama.

BOOSTING CONFIDENCE IN READING

Here are some activities you can do at home to help your child with reading.

How	Why	What You Can DO
Talk about what they read.	Making connections with text helps to broaden the meaning.	Text- to Text Text to World Text to Self
After dinner activity to draw.	Helps your child connect with what they read... and sparks creativity.	Bond with your child by drawing a picture of the story.
Dinner Theater	Helps your child to sequence the story and view reading as fun.	Create a puppet show on the story.

READING LIST FOR KINDERGARTEN

Use this as a starting point for your child's reading log. Add books and dates that it was read.

Clifford Makes a Friend by Norman Bridwell	Date
David Goes to School by David Shannon	Date
	Date
	Date
	Date
	Date
	Date
	Date
	Date

READING LIST FOR GRADE 1

Use this as a starting point for your child's reading log. Add books and dates that it was read.

Fly High, Fly Guy by Tedd Arnold	Date
I Want My Hat Back by Jon Klassen	Date
	Date
	Date
	Date
	Date
	Date
	Date
	Date
	Date

READING LIST FOR GRADE 2

Use this as a starting point for your child's reading log. Add books and dates that it was read.

If You Take a Mouse to School by Laura Numeroff	Date
Polar Bear, Polar Bear What Do You Hear? by Bill Martin	Date
	Date
	Date
	Date
	Date
	Date
	Date
	Date
	Date

READING LIST FOR GRADE 3

Use this as a starting point for your child's reading log. Add books and dates that it was read.

Fly Guy Presents: Weather by Tedd Arnold	Date
Ralph Baer: The Man Behind Video Games by Nancy Dickmann	Date
	Date
	Date
	Date
	Date
	Date
	Date
	Date

READING LIST FOR GRADE 4

Use this as a starting point for your child's reading log. Add books and dates that it was read.

Astronaut in Training by Kathryn Clay	Date
Who is Derek Jeter? by author Gail Herman	Date
	Date
	Date
	Date
	Date
	Date
	Date
	Date
	Date

READING LIST FOR GRADE 5

Use this as a starting point for your child's reading log. Add books and dates that it was read.

Understanding Your Civil Rights by Emma Carlson Berne	Date
What are the Summer Olympics? by Gail Herman	Date
	Date
	Date
	Date
	Date
	Date
	Date
	Date
	Date

What do you do to boost your child's confidence in reading? Explain how and when you will do it.

What 3 things will you differently to partner with your child's teacher? Explain how and when you will do it.

What Not To Do...
when approaching a teacher

Do	Don't
Attend the IEP meeting on time	Forget about it and force someone to hunt you down
Recognize that it is a formal, legal and confidential meeting	Say anything that will come back to haunt you
Assume the teacher knows how the child is doing	Withhold information because you are scared to upset the teacher
Bring data and work samples	Demanding a meeting unannounced during instruction.
Share ideas that might work in class	Feel intimidated or let everyone else make suggestions
Take notes	Accusing the teacher of not liking your child.
Put yourself in the teachers shoes	Do NOT have negative conversations about the teacher at home.
Speak up	Don't accuse the teacher before listening.
Be a team player	Be uncooperative. Display inappropriate behavior.
Share positives about the child	Complain about the child or teacher to the other.
Listen up and ask questions	Contact the principal before speaking to the teacher.
Be willing to try new things	Stick with things that aren't working

What is the best way to approach a teacher?

Teachers receive the same questions a lot...

Here is a list of frequently asked questions with answers to ease your mind.

Frequently Asked Questions

So, which one is my child's teacher?

Both!

Why is my child in this class if my child is not special education?

Your child is in this class because it's an inclusion class. This means special education and general education students are in the same classroom.

What if the pacing is too slow or too fast because of the varying levels?

Because there are extra adults in the room, your child will have the advantage of extra support. This includes hands-on activities and reteaching to connect with the lessons.

Frequently Asked Questions

Is my child like everyone else?

Every child is different and learns differently. Teachers cannot discuss other students. Please schedule a conference to discuss your child's performance and growth.

Is my child behind?

During conferences and communication, the teacher will inform you of your child's current level of performance.

What's the best way to contact the teacher?

Email is the best way to contact a teacher.

What questions do you have for the teacher? Write those concerns here.

What questions do you have for the teacher? Write those concerns here.

8 Questions to ask the teacher

Knowing the right questions to ask is important as how you ask those questions. These 8 questions will help you help your child.

1. What can I do to support my child at home?
2. Do you have examples?
3. Can you send a guide home for me to help?
4. What can I do to help my child?
5. What website can I go to?
6. What time/days are tutorials offered at the school?
7. If not, are you aware of any local programs for tutoring?
8. Can I help my child with their homework?

What questions do you have for the teacher? Write those concerns here.

Questions to Ask in Meetings

1. How can I contact you?

2. When is a good time to have a conversation about my child's progress?

3. What do you see as my child's strengths? How can I support and encourage them?

4. What kind of progress can I expect to see? What will it look like?

5. What can I do *at home* to support our goals?

6. Which of these goals are top priority?

7. How will the progress be measured? How often will we communicate about the progress?

8. What will this support look like on a daily basis? How will my child's day look?

9. What additional resources can I use at home to support my child?

What questions will you ask in the next meeting?

Advocating for Your Child

"Great things in business are never done by one person. They are done by a team of people" - John C. Maxwell

5 Ways to Advocate for Your Child

1. Ask your child about the day

2. Request services

3. Know your school board

4. Partner with the school

5. Become more involved

Ask your child about their day

Asking a child "how was your day?" can be a dead-end question. These 10 questions will help you dig deeper into your child's daily experience at school.

1. Tell me about the best part of your day.

2. What was the hardest thing you did today?

3. Did any of your classmates make you laugh today?

4. Tell me about what you read in class.

5. Who did you play with today? What did you play?

6. Do you think math [or any subject] is too easy or too hard?

7. What's the biggest difference between this year and last year?

8. What rules are different at school than our rules at home? Do you think the rule is fair?

9. Who did you sit with at lunch?

10. Can you show me something you learned (or did) today?

Share some of your child's responses.

Reading Questions

Character

- Who are the characters?
- How do you think the character felt when...
- Do you think the characer would make a good friend? Why or why not?
- How are the characters similar/different to each other?
- Why do you think the character did this?

Plot

- What happened at the begining, middle, end of the story?
- How would you have solved the problem?
- What other ways could the problem have been solved?
- What's the best part in the book? Why?
- How would you change the story?

Reading Questions

Text Connections

- Have you ever met anyone like the character?
- Has something similiar ever happened to you?
- Does this book remind you of any other books you have read? How?
- Could the story happen in real life? Why or why not?

Reading Strategies

- Summarize what happened in the story.
- What do you think is going to happen next?
- Why do you think the author wrote this book?
- Who is telling the story?
- Do you have any more questions about the text?
- What did you picture when you read this part?

Reflection Questions

Ask yourself the following questions.
Take 15 minutes to think and complete.

1. Describe your child's social and academic strengths

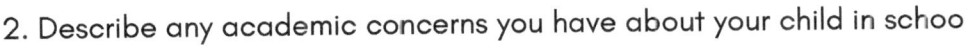

2. Describe any academic concerns you have about your child in school

3. What social or behavioral concerns do you have about your child?

Reflection Questions

Ask yourself the following questions.
Take 15 minutes to think and complete.

4. Is your child able to take care of his/her personal needs?

5. What is the most important goal you would like to see your child accomplish this school year?

6. Are there any concerns that you have?

Reflection Questions

Ask yourself the following questions.
Take 15 minutes to think and complete.

7. What language does your child use to communicate with you?

8. What other languages are spoken at home?

9. Do you need a translated copy of documents?

Notes

A TO Z

List characteristics of parents that are involved in schools. Share one word for each letter.

A	**B**	**C**
D	**E**	**F**
G	**H**	**I**
J	**K**	**L**
M	**N**	**O**
P	**Q**	**R**
S	**T**	**U**
V	**W**	**X**
Y	**Z**	

What can you do differently to become more actively involved? Use the completed A to Z List.

ACTION PLAN

An action plan is a list of the tasks to complete a single goal. Creating your own action plan is the best way to become a more involved parent in your child's education.

Action Item	Date
Action Item	Date
Action Item	Date
Action Item	Date
Action Item	Date
Action Item	Date
Action Item	Date
Action Item	Date
Action Item	Date

Notes from the Action Plan.

Additional Notes
from the Action Plan.

Additional Notes
from the Action Plan.

Benefits of partnering with teachers

Increased appreciation of differences

Increased overall academic achievement

Increased time and attention for your child's education

New and positive lasting friendships

Increased self-esteem and self-worth

Strong sense of a classroom community

Confident child

Increased support for instruction

Meeting Checklist

Main Topic :

Start :

End :

Point Notes

- [ ] **Discuss the main purpose of the meeting**

- [ ] **Ensure the meeting time**

- [ ] **Contact the teacher**

- [ ] **Check the meeting agenda**

- [ ] **Take notes of important points**

- [ ] **Make sure to ask important questions**

- [ ] **Recap the meeting agreements**

Advocating for Your Child

Take massive action!

Advocating for Your Child

Here are some of the ways that you can empower yourself and child with the school district.

1. Gathering and maintaining a contact list for school resources.
2. Offer creative suggestions and solutions to the school. Back it up with research.
3. Ask questions.
4. Share accurate information.
5. Research the resources
6. Find the advocates.

Important Contacts

Build this contact list to advocate for your child.

My Child's Teacher
Name:
Email:

School Nurse
Name:
Email:

Counselor
Name:
Email:

Principal
Name:
Email:

District Superintendent

Name:
Email:

School Board Members

Name:
Email:

Name:
Email:

Name:
Email:

Name:
Email:

Tutoring Groups

Name:
Phone:

Name:
Phone:

MEETING NOTES

ATTENDEES

DATE

_____

_____

_____

NOTES

_____

_____

AGENDA

_____

_____

_____

ACTION PLAN

TASKS	TASKS OWNER	TIMELINE

Record your thoughts
after each parent-teacher interaction

One thing I want to remember about today...

....

....

Today I felt...

....

....

Today I'm grateful for...

....

....

I want to learn more about...

....

....

MEETING NOTES

ATTENDEES

DATE

_____

_____

_____

_____

NOTES

_____

_____

_____

_____

_____

AGENDA

_____

_____

_____

_____

_____

_____

_____

_____

_____

_____

_____

_____

_____

ACTION PLAN

TASKS	TASKS OWNER	TIMELINE

Record your thoughts
after each parent-teacher interaction

One thing I want to remember about today...

⋯⋯⋯⋯⋯⋯⋯⋯⋯⋯⋯⋯⋯⋯⋯⋯⋯⋯⋯⋯⋯⋯⋯⋯⋯⋯

⋯⋯⋯⋯⋯⋯⋯⋯⋯⋯⋯⋯⋯⋯⋯⋯⋯⋯⋯⋯⋯⋯⋯⋯⋯⋯

Today I felt...

⋯⋯⋯⋯⋯⋯⋯⋯⋯⋯⋯⋯⋯⋯⋯⋯⋯⋯⋯⋯⋯⋯⋯⋯⋯⋯

⋯⋯⋯⋯⋯⋯⋯⋯⋯⋯⋯⋯⋯⋯⋯⋯⋯⋯⋯⋯⋯⋯⋯⋯⋯⋯

Today I'm grateful for...

⋯⋯⋯⋯⋯⋯⋯⋯⋯⋯⋯⋯⋯⋯⋯⋯⋯⋯⋯⋯⋯⋯⋯⋯⋯⋯

⋯⋯⋯⋯⋯⋯⋯⋯⋯⋯⋯⋯⋯⋯⋯⋯⋯⋯⋯⋯⋯⋯⋯⋯⋯⋯

I want to learn more about...

⋯⋯⋯⋯⋯⋯⋯⋯⋯⋯⋯⋯⋯⋯⋯⋯⋯⋯⋯⋯⋯⋯⋯⋯⋯⋯

⋯⋯⋯⋯⋯⋯⋯⋯⋯⋯⋯⋯⋯⋯⋯⋯⋯⋯⋯⋯⋯⋯⋯⋯⋯⋯

MEETING NOTES

ATTENDEES

DATE

_____

_____

NOTES

AGENDA

ACTION PLAN

TASKS	TASKS OWNER	TIMELINE

Record your thoughts
after each parent-teacher interaction

One thing I want to remember about today...

....

....

Today I felt...

....

....

Today I'm grateful for...

....

....

I want to learn more about...

....

....

MEETING NOTES

ATTENDEES

_____
_____
_____
_____
_____
_____
_____

AGENDA

_____
_____
_____
_____
_____
_____
_____
_____

DATE

_____
_____

NOTES

_____
_____
_____
_____
_____
_____
_____
_____
_____
_____

ACTION PLAN

TASKS	TASKS OWNER	TIMELINE

Record your thoughts
after each parent-teacher interaction

One thing I want to remember about today...

· ·

· ·

Today I felt...

· ·

· ·

Today I'm grateful for...

· ·

· ·

I want to learn more about...

· ·

· ·

MEETING NOTES

ATTENDEES

_____

_____

_____

_____

_____

_____

_____

DATE

_____

_____

NOTES

_____

_____

_____

_____

_____

_____

_____

AGENDA

_____

_____

_____

_____

_____

_____

_____

_____

_____

_____

_____

_____

_____

_____

_____

ACTION PLAN

TASKS	TASKS OWNER	TIMELINE

MEETING NOTES

ATTENDEES

_____

_____

_____

_____

DATE

_____

_____

NOTES

_____

_____

_____

_____

_____

AGENDA

_____

_____

_____

_____

_____

_____

_____

_____

_____

_____

_____

_____

_____

_____

_____

_____

_____

_____

ACTION PLAN

TASKS	TASKS OWNER	TIMELINE

Record your thoughts
after each parent-teacher interaction

One thing I want to remember about today...

· ·

· ·

Today I felt...

· ·

· ·

Today I'm grateful for...

· ·

· ·

I want to learn more about...

· ·

· ·

MEETING NOTES

ATTENDEES

DATE

_____

_____

NOTES

AGENDA

ACTION PLAN

TASKS	TASKS OWNER	TIMELINE

Record your thoughts
after each parent-teacher interaction

One thing I want to remember about today...

....

....

Today I felt...

....

....

Today I'm grateful for...

....

....

I want to learn more about...

....

....

MEETING NOTES

ATTENDEES

DATE

_____

_____

_____

_____

NOTES

_____

_____

_____

_____

AGENDA

_____

_____

_____

_____

_____

_____

_____

_____

_____

_____

_____

_____

_____

_____

ACTION PLAN

TASKS	TASKS OWNER	TIMELINE

Record your thoughts
after each parent-teacher interaction

One thing I want to remember about today...

....

....

Today I felt...

....

....

Today I'm grateful for...

....

....

I want to learn more about...

....

....

MEETING NOTES

ATTENDEES

DATE

_____

_____

_____

_____

NOTES

_____

_____

_____

_____

_____

AGENDA

_____

_____

_____

_____

_____

_____

_____

_____

_____

_____

_____

ACTION PLAN

TASKS	TASKS OWNER	TIMELINE

Record your thoughts
after each parent-teacher interaction

One thing I want to remember about today...

....

....

Today I felt...

....

....

Today I'm grateful for...

....

....

I want to learn more about...

....

....

What's in it for you?

The effects of parental involvement on student achievement are clear: family involvement increases the likelihood that students will graduate, improve their grades, have better attendance, and go to college.

What's in it for you?

Simply put, you will have pride in knowing that you positively impact your child's education, success and overall confidence in learning new things.

Challenge for all parents

If and when you become discouraged with a school or teacher, please remember:

Parent involvement in education is crucial. No matter their background, **students with involved parents are more likely to** have higher grades and test scores, **attend school regularly, have better social skills, show improved behavior, and adapt well to school.**

Challenge for all parents

Your active involvement in your child's education makes the world a better place.

Your involvement means a fresh start for your child. That student will learn to make smarter decisions, navigate life's challenges, and achieve goals that seem larger than life.

I challenge you to stay involved.

References

Covey, Stephen R. (2013). 7 Habits of highly effective people. Simon & Schuster LTD.

Marenus, M. (1970, January 1). [Gardner's theory of multiple intelligences]. https://www.simplypsychology.org/multiple-intelligences.html.

Maxwell, J. (2001). John C. Maxwell quotes. Brainy Quote. https://www.brainyquote.com/quotes/john_c_maxwell_600865

Reading Rockets. (nd). www.readingrockets.org/article/9-components-effective-research-supported-reading

Sasa, T. (2020). Michelle Obama quotes True Leadership, Women Empowerment, and Education. Legit. ng - Nigeria news. https://www.legit.ng/1317329-25-michelle-obama-quotes-education-feminism-leadership.html

www.ingramcontent.com/pod-product-compliance
Lightning Source LLC
Chambersburg PA
CBHW080843120626
46553CB00009B/2552